EXHIBIT RULES

TIPS, RULES, AND TACTICS FOR PREPARING, OFFERING, AND OPPOSING EXHIBITS

SECOND EDITION

D0144174

NATIONAL INSTITUTE FOR TRIAL ADVOCACY

Exhibit Rules

Tips, Rules, and Tactics for Preparing, Offering, and Opposing Exhibits

Second Edition

David Malone

Paul Zwier

Address inquiries to:

Reprint Permission
National Institute for Trial Advocacy
1685 38th Street, Suite 200
Boulder, CO 80301-2735
Phone: (800) 225-6482
Fax: (720) 890-7069
E-mail: permissions@nita.org

ISBN 978-1-60156-196-1

FBA 1196

Library of Congress Cataloging-in-Publication Data

Malone, David M., 1944-

  Exhibit rules : tips, rules, and tactics for preparing, offering, and opposing exhibits / David Malone, Paul Zwier. -- Second Edition.

    pages cm

  ISBN 978-1-60156-196-1

1. Evidence (Law)--United States. 2. Trial practice--United States. I. Zwier, Paul J., 1954- II. Title.

  KF8936.M35 2013

  347.73'6--dc23

                          2012047485

CONTENTS

Chapter One—Foundation for Exhibits

**Chapter Two—Foundation for Specific
Exhibits**

**Chapter Three—Common Problems
with Graphic Exhibits**

**Chapter Four—Handling Documents
in Court**

**Chapter Five—Choosing the Medium
and the Occasion**

Chapter Six—Experts and Exhibits

Chapter Seven—Evidentiary Principles for Certain Types of Documents

Chapter Eight—Exhibits Divulged or Obtained as Part of Mandatory "Voluntary" Pretrial Disclosures and other Discovery

Chapter Nine—The Mechanics of Pretrial Listings and Pretrial Rulings on Exhibits

Chapter Ten—The Next Level of Persuasion with Exhibits

CHAPTER ONE

FOUNDATION FOR EXHIBITS

1.1 The OPRAH Elements

The five elements of foundation are:

- original document rule;

- privilege;

- relevance;

- authenticity; and

- hearsay.

Use the mnemonic "OPRAH" to remember these five elements. These are the only elements of foundation for exhibits. Normally, only two or three of these elements are involved in laying the foundation for the admission of an item of evidence. For example, Mickey Mantle's #7 game shirt would be admissible based on testimony that he wore it (authenticity) and because it helps resolve the issue in the lawsuit between the sports memorabilia collectors of whether his number was "7" or "6" in 1951, his first year (relevance).[1] Thus, the only foundational elements necessary in that case are authenticity and relevance.

OPRAH is a convenient way to remember these elements of foundation, but according to the order of the frequency with which they are encountered and in which they should be analyzed on your or your opponent's exhibits, it should be RAHPO: every item of admitted evidence must be relevant, and it must be authentic, what it is purported to be—that is, it can't be a forgery or shown to be fraudulently created; hearsay comes up very often, because almost every document in litigation has a potential hearsay problem (statements made out of court, offered for truth); privilege comes up often,

---

1. "The Mick" actually came up to the Big Leagues with the Yankees twice, and the first time up he wore #6; he did not perform especially well and was sent down to the minors; when he came back up, later that same year, he wore #7.

although normally in pretrial during discovery and the subsequent arguments about documents; and the original document rules comes up very, very rarely, primarily because of the availability of "duplicate originals," discussed below.

1.2 Original Document Rule

The **"Original Document Rule,"** sometimes called the "Best Evidence Rule," has nothing to do with the *quality* of the evidence being offered. This rule is concerned only with whether an offered document is an original or a copy. This rule is embodied in Federal Rules of Evidence 1002–04. It states that if a document is being offered to prove its contents, and those contents are closely related to the resolution of an important or controlling issue in the case, then the original of the document should be presented or its absence explained: "It was burned," "It is in the possession of the opponent who has not produced it after request," or "It is lost," are examples.

1.3 Duplicate Originals

"Duplicate" originals are as admissible as the original document itself. "Originals" include—as "duplicate originals"—photographic and xerographic counterparts, counterparts produced simultaneously with the original (such as carbon copies), computer-generated counterparts, and any other counterparts produced in a manner assuring accuracy and genuineness. Of course, if the primary original was signed and the signature is significant to the use of the document in the lawsuit, then unsigned duplicate originals would not be "originals" to prove any signature; but they would be treated as originals to show the contents of the original. This rule regarding duplicate originals is sufficiently flexible to be applied to new forms of duplicate originals as technology progresses. When the rule was drafted, facsimile machines were not widely used, but faxes clearly qualify as duplicate originals today, as do electronic or digital copies, pictures on cell phones, and screen shots; computer files can be printed multiple times—each is identical and thus a duplicate original; scanned documents also become duplicate originals. The fact that a document is an original or a duplicate original under this rule does not itself satisfy any hearsay problems. We may agree that we are looking at the original of the book the storekeeper used to enter transactions, so there is no original document rule problem, but the "business records exception" to the rule excluding hearsay requires more than that to show that the entries in the book are sufficiently trustworthy to fit within the exception (Rule 803(6)—Records of a Regularly Conducted Activity).

1.4   When an Original Is Not Required

If the contents of the document are not important to resolving issues in the case, an original will not be required. The original document rule embodies a preference for the most reliable proof of a document's contents that is practicably available, but the emphasis is on "practicably." The requirements of this rule will give way readily to considerations of avoiding confusion and waste of time.

1.5   No Preferred Status

If an original is not available, secondary proof may be admitted, and there is no hierarchy to the secondary proof of the document's contents. Once the court has determined that there is a satisfactory explanation for the absence of the original (including any duplicate originals), the proponent may offer secondary evidence of the contents: testimony, other documents, or circumstantial evidence. There is no preferred status given to any of these other methods of proof. Thus, if a letter is important to an issue in the case and no original (or duplicate original) is available, a witness could testify about what he read in the letter (but not what it meant if the meaning is parole evidence), or a draft could be introduced, or the reaction of the recipient could be described as a basis for inferring the contents ("He read the letter, then immediately started to cry and said, 'I have to go home to my dog's funeral.'").

1.6 When Oral Evidence Is Not Precluded

When testimony is offered to describe a historical incident, the fact that the incident may have been recorded in a document does not activate the Original Document Rule to preclude the oral testimony. The mere fact that an event has been captured in a document does not mean that other evidence is less acceptable or admissible. For example, an eyewitness to the funeral of President Kennedy can testify about what he saw, even though those events were also recorded in thousands of newspaper articles; an astronaut can testify about what he saw on the surface of the moon, even though movie cameras recorded every instant. In these examples, the attempt is to prove the event, not to prove the content of the document; indeed, the fact that a document records the event is only coincidental.

1.7 Rarity of Successful Original Documents Rule Challenge

Original document problems are rare. Of all of the problems of foundation, those involving best evidence considerations are the most infrequent.[2] Consider all of the other elements of foundation

---

2. The author has made one original document objection in court in forty-two years of practice: the opponent tried to obtain testimony about the actual regulations on fire detectors from the National Bureau of Standards, which were published in a booklet. The writing was the subject of the testimony, not any incident. The court precluded the testimony since no showing had been made that the printed standards were unavailable.

before seeking to satisfy or base a challenge on the original document or best evidence rule.

1.8 Authentication

"**Authentication**" refers to the process of showing that the item of evidence is in fact what the proponent claims that it is. Thus, if an item is offered as the jewelry box in which Grandma kept her brooch, there must be some proof that it is *in fact* that box—testimony from someone who saw Grandma take her brooch from the box, or a document, perhaps a photograph, that provides a description of the box.

1.9 Authentication and Oral Testimony

Authentication applies to documentary and real evidence, but it does not normally apply in that same sense to live witness testimony. A document offered as the Last Will and Testament of John Adams must be shown, by direct or circumstantial evidence, to be that document; a buyer's signature must be shown to have been written by that buyer. Grandma's brooch box needs authenticating evidence through testimonial or documentary evidence; but the testimony of a witness in court is not "authenticated" by extrinsic evidence that the witness is who she says she is. Instead, we allow examination on whether the witness is competent. In this context, competency means that the witness is speaking of matters that the witness perceived or are within an expert's field of demonstrated expertise. (The broader meaning of witness competence includes the ability to comprehend the oath, the ability to recall, the ability to recount, and the ability to perceive.)[3] A competent witness could authenticate a signature by testifying that he saw the person actually sign it. Otherwise, courts can authenticate signatures by getting an expert to compare the signature with

---

3. The testimony of expert witnesses requires authentication in one sense to be admissible: the court must be satisfied that the witness and the methodology employed are both reliable—that is, are capable of producing accurate results—so that the opinions expressed represent (that is, are authenticated as) knowledge, rather than folklore, religious belief, superstition, or unscientific-based suppositions or speculation. In this sense, the expert opinion testimony must be authenticated before it is admitted. This specialized foundation for expert testimony is fully explored in the companion books *Expert Rules* and *Effective Expert Testimony*. Obviously, these are not "exhibit" problems.

a known exemplar. Or the judge could make the comparison for him or herself.[4]

1.10 Relevance

"Relevance" is a necessary element of the foundation for any item of evidence. If an item of documentary or physical evidence is not relevant, it is not coming into evidence, no matter how many of the other four elements of foundation it satisfies.

1.11 Relevance Defined

Relevance is the tendency of any item of evidence—real, documentary, or testimonial—to make a fact at issue more or less likely than that fact would be without the evidence. Rule 401 contains this definition, and it is followed across most state jurisdictions. Relevance is determined by the facts at issue, and the facts at issue are determined by the complaint, answer, and witness credibility. For example, in a contract matter, the facts at issue are whether a contract was formed, whether a contract

4. Fed. R. Evid. 901(b).

was breached, whether there were damages from the breach, and whether witnesses are telling the truth. If the document offered is a letter from the defendant advising his friend that he cannot take a weekend trip because he has promised to paint the plaintiff's house, this letter is relevant because it makes more likely the existence of the contract asserted in the complaint. In the same case, a picture of the plaintiff in a wheelchair with a leg cast and a neck brace taken a week before the contract was allegedly created would probably not, without more, be relevant. Attempts to get the picture into evidence by seeking to ask the defendant whether this was the person with whom he discussed house painting should be seen as a sham by the court (when analyzed under Rule 403 as causing more confusion than its minimal probative value justifies), because identity was not actually placed in issue by the pleadings. If the court does not agree with that analysis, the defendant can simplify it—in this case by offering to stipulate to the identity of the plaintiff, thereby clearly taking the fact out of issue and rendering the picture irrelevant because identity has been established. While more complex cases may extend this analysis, the principles remain the same: evidence is relevant only to facts that are in issue. Remember, however, that witness credibility is always in issue. Thus, exhibits that are used to impeach or rehabilitate a witness's testimony are relevant.

1.12 Authentic and Relevant Documents May Be Excluded

Exhibits that are authentic and relevant may be excluded because of other evidentiary or policy considerations. Authentic and relevant exhibits may violate rules controlling hearsay; invade a privilege; or be adjudged to create a danger of unfair prejudice, confusion, or delay that outweighs their probative value.[5]

---

5. FED. R. EVID. 403 contains an exclusionary rule, which is an appeal to the discretion of the court. Despite the proscription against speaking objections and the legitimate preference for short-form objections, it is difficult to state this objection in court without "talking it" on the one hand or sounding to the jury like a stuffy lawyer on the other. A reasonable compromise might be: "Objection under Rule 403. Unfairly prejudicial." If the judge continues to look at you, continue with: "This exhibit is so unfair that its minimal probative value is not sufficient to justify admitting it into the record."

1.13 Privilege

The law of privilege is supplied by whatever jurisdiction supplies the substantive law of decision on the issue to which the exhibit is relevant. Rule 501 does not attempt to list federal or other privileges, as some state codes of evidence do. It instead provides this "choice of law" rule, which is significant in diversity and pendant or ancillary jurisdiction cases in federal courts. In general, federal privileges are common law rather than statutory. There is, for example, no federal privilege for communications between accountants and clients (although such a privilege is often proposed by the major accounting firms). However, there are states—such as Maryland—that specifically recognize such a privilege. Thus, in a diversity case based on Maryland civil conspiracy law, the privilege would apply to protect a company's accounting communications from disclosure, while in a federal racketeering and conspiracy case brought in Maryland federal court, no privilege would apply to protect such communications[6]

---

6. If documents claimed to be work-product or covered by attorney-client privilege are turned over, intentionally

1.14 Effect of Privilege on Laying Foundation

If the foundation for a document demonstrates the existence of a privilege, the court may exclude the document. "Nonprivileged" is the only element of foundation for which the burden (of showing privilege) is on the party opposing admission—that is, the opposing party must show the existence of a privilege. On this element, if there is no evidence of privilege, the document is admissible (assuming that the other elements of foundation have been established). With respect to the other elements—original document, authenticity, relevance, and hearsay—the proponent bears the burden (of showing that the document is original, is authentic, is relevant, and is not excluded by the rule excluding hearsay) and the offer will

---

or inadvertently, the disclosing attorney's opportunity to retrieve them is covered by FED. R. EVID. 502 and FED. R. CIV. P. 26(b)(5)(B), as amended in 2011 and 2010, respectively. In essence, "claw-back" of inadvertently disclosed materials is allowed if timely notice is given of the disclosure and privilege. The receiving party must return, destroy, or sequester the materials until the court can rule on the claim of privilege.

fail if that threshold showing is insufficient. Most privilege problems in civil litigation are resolved in the pretrial phase. Questions concerning attorney-client privilege, accountant-client privilege, self-investigation privilege, doctor-patient privilege, attorney work product doctrine, spiritual advisor-penitent privilege, or husband-wife or marital privilege can arise in criminal proceedings where there is little opportunity for pretrial resolution, and the criminal defense attorney needs to be on guard for these. Also she should be on guard for the offer of evidence that invades client's rights of privacy or would violate trade secrets or protective orders.

1.15 Hearsay

"Hearsay" is a problem if a document contains a statement that was made out of court and is offered for its truth. In those circumstances, the "hearsay rule" (or, technically, the rule excluding hearsay) may apply to render the document inadmissible (or at least the portion of it containing the hearsay statement). Although this rule is stated as though there were just two elements to the definition of hearsay—"out of court" and "offered for the truth"—there are actually three elements, because the evidentiary material must also constitute a *statement*, that is, it must be intended by the declarant, the "stating" person, as a statement which depends on his credibility. To use a common example, if a witness testifies that he knew it was raining because he saw people through the window with umbrellas up, the testimony would be admissible over a hearsay objection because the people outside did not intend their activity as a statement and their behavior was a circumstance that the witness could use as one basis for concluding that it was raining. However, if the witness testifies that he asked his friend to open his umbrella outside the window if the bus appeared at the end of the street, then the friend's action was intended by the friend to constitute a statement ("the bus is almost here!"), and we are concerned because we do not have the friend, the maker of the statement (the declarant), on the stand for cross-examination. In short, if the exhibit is intended to take the place of speech, it will be judged as hearsay. Do not forget that internal statements in graphic exhibits—statements indicating amounts, dates, sources limitations, or time periods, for example—are generally, and correctly, considered out-of-court statements offered for their truth.[7]

1.16   Hearsay Exceptions

The exceptions (found in Federal Rules of Evidence 803 and 804) to the rule excluding hearsay, in exhibits or otherwise, are construed strictly and conservatively. Since the codification of the federal rules of evidence, no new exceptions have been created in the federal system, and the existing exceptions have been fairly consistently interpreted to reject expansion.[8] In general, the courts

---

7. Many such exhibits with embedded hearsay actually constitute "summary exhibits" under FED. R. EVID. 1006, where the hearsay contained in the exhibit's sourcing, data, or marking is essentially "cured" by requiring disclosure of the underlying data a reasonable time before use in court. The offered summary exhibit stands in the place of the underlying data, which may need a hearsay exception of its own, like learned treatises (Rule 803(18)), or market reports (Rule 803(17)). In other words, the document, created outside of court, makes a statement, and that statement itself contains a statement, which is hearsay. *See* FED. R. EVID. 805, "Hearsay Within Hearsay," and text at 1.17.

8. *But see* United States v. Lasiter, 258 F. 3d 525 (6th Cir. 2001) (where the court in a criminal case alleging that

have proclaimed that the exceptions will be strictly construed so that circumstances that come close to satisfying an exception, but fail to meet the specific requirements of the rule, will not be approved under that exception or under the residual or "catch-all" exception now contained in Rule 807 (previously Rules 803(24) and 804(b)(5)). There is a genuine concern that unless these exceptions are kept within their traditional bounds, they will swallow the rule excluding hearsay, which is founded in ancient principles preserving the preference for live testimony. The catch-all exception is intended to allow courts to exercise some discretion when faced with unusual circumstances beyond the contemplation of the drafters of the original rules—not for circumstances that the

---

the defendant was manufacturing methamphetamine, let in financial records of the defendant through the testimony of an investigator who was unable to lay the foundation for a business record under FED. R. EVID. 803(6). It found that the trustworthiness of the document was established under the requirements of FED. R. EVID. 807, known as the "catch-all" exception.

drafters could have included, but chose not to.[9]
If you intend to rely on Rule 807, you need to
give your opponent notice (including name and
address of the declarant offering the evidence)
before the hearing to give your opponent a fair
opportunity to meet the offer with an objection.

1.17 Exhibits

Exhibits often present hearsay problems because
they summarize out-of-court statements or use
them as sources. You cannot eliminate hearsay
problems merely by incorporating the data into
another exhibit. While exhibits may be specially
prepared and offered as summaries of complex
or voluminous underlying data or material—
accounting, economic, and scientific graphs or
video demonstrations and re-creations being prime
examples—the summary exhibit incorporates all
of the hearsay deficiencies contained within the
underlying data. Thus, hearsay rules apply to the

---

9. To take advantage of the Rule 807 catch-all exception,
the proponent needs to give the opponent notice, pretrial,
that he will use FED. R. EVID. 807 as a basis for admissibility
of the proffered hearsay evidence.

summary exhibits. As a corollary, when evaluating an opponent's exhibits, independently consider the foundation for all data underlying summary exhibits. Market reports and commercial publications containing such summaries may meet Rule 803(17) if they are contained in publications relied on by the public or persons in particular occupations.

1.18 Exhibit Used to Impeach, Refresh Recollection, or as Past Recollection Recorded

An exhibit used to impeach a witness, to refresh recollection, or as past recollection recorded is read to the witness and into the record, but the document itself is not received or provided to the jury. Because an exhibit is being offered either as a substitute for or in contrast to the witness's testimony, it is received orally, just like the witness's testimony. This is so the jury is not led to place inappropriate weight on a testimonial substitute merely because it was transcribed to or originally appeared on a piece of paper. The concept here (inadmissibility of the underlying document) is identical for all exhibits intended to refresh memory or stand in place of the witness's testimony (and, for that matter, for learned treatises under Rule 803(18), which may supplement or contradict an expert's testimony).

1.19   Rule of Completeness

If part of an exhibit is accepted into evidence—as substantive evidence or solely for impeachment—the opponent may offer other portions that the jury, in fairness, should consider at the same time. Rule 106, the "rule of completeness," is intended to prevent an advocate from misleading the jury by presenting only a portion of an exhibit. The proper functioning of the rule permits the opponent to request that the court authorize the admission of the additional portions at the same time, so that the jury has the complete context. In practice, however, courts often respond to such requests by stating, "Well, you have cross-examination." Of course you have cross-examination; you had it without Rule 106, so such a ruling ignores the important purpose of the rule, which is putting the two statements together in time when the jury can most easily judge the relationship between them. If the document in question is a formal deposition, then Rule 32(a)(4) performs the same function. When arguing for the admission of additional portions of a deposition, cite both Rule 106 and Rule 32(a)(4). Note, however, if you are offering deposition testimony of an unavailable witness against a defendant in a criminal case, such an offer may violate the defendant's Sixth Amendment rights to confront that witness in court, and the testimony would be inadmissible on that basis.

Chapter Two

Foundation for Specific Exhibits

2.1 Photographs

A photograph is admissible on a showing that it fairly and accurately depicts a relevant scene at a relevant time. Focus your analysis of the foundation for photographic evidence on whether the photograph fairly and accurately depicts the relevant view as seen by the witness. Therefore, it does not matter whether the exhibit was photographed (or recorded by whatever process) at a relevant time (any more than a chart prepared for an accountant's testimony must have been prepared at the same time that the sales and revenues were earned). The important question for both the photograph and the accounting testimony is whether someone familiar with the "view" is able to testify in court that the relevant scene is accurately and fairly presented.

2.2 Admissibility of Photographs, Movies, and Computer Graphics

Photographs, movies, and computer graphics are admissible if they are fair, accurate, and relevant. (For simplicity, let's call them all "photographs" here—unless there is a distinction to be made.) If the individual "frame" of a graphic exhibit is fair and accurate, the exhibit is ordinarily admissible. This is equally true of the thousands of frames that comprise a motion picture as of the single frame that comprises a still photograph, unless there is something about the motion—perhaps the speed—that renders the series of frames unfair (under Rule 403). For example, a video of a police officer arresting a suspect might, when played at normal speed, accurately show the events that led to the policeman using his baton to subdue the person. However H, if the video were shown at slow speed, it might give the appearance that the policeman had more time to control the person without the use of force than was in fact the case.

Similarly, any cropping or enlargement or enhancement of photographs—stills or motion— might place undue emphasis on certain portions of the picture or scene, just as omitting portions of a document might result in an unfair or incomplete understanding of the document. This is obviously true even when the original pictures are themselves fair and accurate. A simple solution here is to require that the scene be presented in "normal" size, without cropping, alongside the enlarged or cropped portion. This way, the jurors can determine for themselves whether the altered scene is fair. When a witness has testified that a depiction is fair and accurate, the burden of challenging that foundation shifts to the opponent, who must present some evidence that the depiction is unfair itself or has been presented or altered in some unfair way. Where the opponent challenges the admissibility of a photograph, movie, or computer simulation on the basis that the witness lacks competence to testify that it is relevant—where he cannot say that he ever had a similar view, that the actors and their actions were reasonably similar to the actual parties involved, or that the facts entered in the mathematical model were accurate and complete—in other words, he cannot say that it is relevant to any issue in the case, then the admissibility question is handled under Rule 104(b). The relevancy is conditioned on a fact, and the proponent only needs to provide evidence that would support a finding that the witness had the perspective to say that the exhibit is fair and accurate for it to be admissible. The rest of the challenge goes to weight.

Determinations of preliminary matters regarding admissibility are conducted out of the hearing of the jury, under Rule 104(c). Some judges are more skeptical about admitting movies and computer simulations than they are about admitting photographs because computer and motion picture evidence make a much stronger impression on the jury and because they too have seen the magic that Spielberg can create. The relevance and reliability analysis some courts apply to computer and motion picture evidence is analogous to the process for evaluating the admissibility of expert testimony under *Daubert* and *Kumho*. Remember that under *Daubert*, the court acts as a gatekeeper, determining as a foundational and preliminary matter whether the methodology controlled for enough of the important variables, has been subjected to critique from peers in the field, can be replicated by others in the field, has a knowable error rate, or meets other criteria of reliability. In other words, these courts treat the admissibility question as though the exhibit had to be absolutely free from any possibility of unfairness in interpretation or use.

Other judges instead treat movies and computer simulations just like single-frame photos. They hear arguments that refer to four rules: Rule 403 states that evidence that causes unfair prejudice, confusion, or delay may be excluded, even if relevant; Rule 102 states that the rules of evidence are to be construed to secure fairness, eliminate unjustifiable expense and delay, and promote the growth of the law of evidence to the end that the truth may be ascertained; Rule 104(b) requires that admissibility be founded on evidence sufficient to support a finding; and Rule 611(a) establishes the court's control over the mode and order of presentation of witnesses and evidence to facilitate finding the truth and avoid wasting time. Thus, if a still picture is admissible because it avoids wasting time (and introducing the thousands of words they replace), movies and computer simulations should be doubly and triply so. Many courts have recognized that technological presentations can produce substantive evidence.

2.3 Admissibility of Video

Video, on disk, tape, or chip, requires the same foundation as standard motion pictures. The technology employed in making the record—in creating the visual exhibit—is not an element of the foundation itself, but it may be relevant in persuading the court that the depiction is not fair and accurate because the process was subject to abuse and was, in fact, abused. However, unless there is some showing that the particular video process can be more easily altered than normal photographic motion pictures, the analysis of admissibility will be the same for either technology. If the challenge to admissibility is based on a claim of alteration, then differences in the ability to alter the pictures would be relevant.

2.4 Admissibility of Reenactments

Photographs and movies of a *reenactment* are admissible if they are "fair and accurate" and the scene is relevant. In other words, if there is evidence that the signing of the Declaration of

Independence looked "just like" it looks in this photograph or that movie and the particulars of the scene are relevant to the case, it will be admissible. The more important the particulars of the scene are, the more demanding the court's admissibility analysis will be. This rule flows from the basic evidentiary requirement that the recorded evidence be a fair depiction; for example, if the witness can testify that the reenactment fairly and accurately depicts the relevant scene as that witness saw it, at the level of the relevant details, then the fact that it is a reenactment is irrelevant.

For example, the actors in the movie portraying the participants in the events at suit are not themselves vouching for the accuracy of their actions or the accuracy of the entire resulting scene; that depends on the sponsoring witness's testimony about the fairness and accuracy of the depiction. The analysis of a computer-generated reenactment is conceptually more difficult, because often there is no one who can testify directly as to the fairness and accuracy of the scene shown. For example, a computer-generated re-creation may be used to show the locations and movements of all the vehicles relevant to a traffic accident, perhaps from an overhead perspective unavailable to any person at the time of the accident. Here, the fairness and accuracy of the computer-generated re-creation depends on the testimony of a witness who is familiar with or participated in the preparation of the re-enactment. If that witness can identify bases for the computer inputs (data), and he (or another witness) is able to testify about the reliability of the methodology (the computer programs) used to generate the re-creation from that data, then the fairness and accuracy of the computer-generated evidence will have been established. By analogy, we accept expert testimony that acid added to a basic solution results in a number of hydrogen ions (H-) combining with hydroxyl ions (OH+), forming neutral water (H_2O) and releasing hydrogen gas, even though the chemist does not actually see the interaction between the molecules and their electrons. The key to admissibility is the demonstration of the reliability of the methodology employed, as emphasized by the Supreme Court in *Daubert v. Merrill-Dow Pharmaceuticals, Inc.*[1] If the methodology—here, the computer

---

1. 509 U.S. 579 (1993).

program—is shown to be reliable, and if the data input are shown to be reliable, and if the scene is relevant, then the visual re-creation or reenactment will be admissible, even though no human being ever actually saw the events depicted.

2.5 Admissibility of Computer-Generated Simulations or Reenactments

Computer-generated simulations or reenactments are admissible if they are fair, accurate, and relevant depictions, but the possibility of improper manipulation (through computer technology) will have to be addressed. Because technology is now available to alter photographs and videos at a very fine level (that is, by changing individual pixels, the small elements which, when combined in groups of hundreds of thousands, form the picture), the proponent of the visual evidence must allay the skepticism jurors or the court may feel toward important visual evidence. While the jurors do not have the opportunity to rule on accepting the evidence into the record, they certainly decide whether to accept the evidence into their deliberations. Those concerns may persuade the proponent to ask at least a few questions to demonstrate through the witness that there has been no tampering. As a matter of presentation, these questions should be in the form of, "Has anyone had an opportunity to manipulate either the data or the program?" rather than, "How do you know that the data are accurate and that they were accurately handled?" because the latter formulation presents too direct a challenge to the testimony of the proponent's own witness.

2.6   Competent Witnesses

Anyone who viewed the actual scene at a relevant time can testify about the fairness and accuracy of the visual evidence. There is no requirement that the foundational witness be a party to the lawsuit or, alternatively, that the witness be uninvolved in the lawsuit. The only requirement for a foundational witness is that she was able to perceive the relevant scene at a relevant time (or, in the case of computer-generated evidence, that she have the competence to testify about the reliability of the program used and the data input). We test the foundational witness's competence to lay the foundation for visual evidence in the same way that we test her ability to testify directly to the scene which she saw: if she can say, "Then I saw him lift the baseball bat over his head," she will also be allowed to say, "This picture of him fairly and accurately shows the way in which he lifted the bat over his head." In the computer-generated evidence context, if the foundational witness would be allowed to testify that in her opinion, the processes would have certain results, then she will also be allowed to testify that a visual exhibit showing those results is fair and accurate. Note that a "relevant time" for viewing in the eyewitness context may be *any time* the scene appeared in the same condition as it did when the lawsuit incident occurred. So if the intersection collision occurred on a dry, moonless night, then a witness who viewed the intersection on any dry, moonless night could supply foundational testimony for a photograph. Indeed, it could even be a photograph of another intersection—if the witness says that it "fairly and accurately" looks like the intersection in question, then that portion of the foundation will be considered as having been established.

2.7   Connecting Data Input

Data *input* must often be connected by technical testimony to the exhibit that shows data or graphic *output*. For example, if the actual scene was not witnessed or could not be witnessed—the scene is a view of the inside of an operating nuclear reactor, for example—foundation evidence will need to include technical testimony to show that a reliable methodology has converted the data input into the data or graphic output (consistent with *Daubert v. Merrill-Dow*). As other examples, statistical regression analyses performed by computer, or DNA comparisons shown on charts, or chemical analyses displayed in summary charts have to be founded on testimony about the reliability of the methodology used to manipulate and display the data.

2.8   Medical Imaging

X-rays and other medical images (CAT scans, MRIs) require foundational evidence linking the particular film or digital record to the specific patient. This is a matter of simple authentication, nothing more. "Is this in fact the image of Julia

O'Brien's fractured vertebrae?"[2] The technology of the x-ray process has been sufficiently established over the years that courts no longer require any expert testimony to demonstrate that there is a reasonable basis for believing that what is seen is actually what is inside the patient's leg. In contrast, however, consider magnetic resonance images (MRI) and CAT scans. A court may require some foundational evidence on the simple fact that this image came from that patient, but also on the more complex fact that this process is showing something that is actually inside the patient. (The question of whether the image shown in fact is useful goes to its relevance, the other portion of the *Daubert-Kumho* "reliability-relevance" or "foundation and fit" requirement.)

---

2. The question for the judge, in technical terms, is actually, "Could a reasonable jury, on this foundational evidence, find that this is in fact the image of Julia O'Brien's fractured vertebrae?" The judge does not determine whether the jury must find that it is that image—that would be a directed verdict standard. This admissibility standard is the lowest threshold at trial.

2.9 Unique Identification and Chain of Custody

Evidence that possesses substantive value because it is the particular item used in the relevant event—such as the weapon used in an assault—needs to be connected by evidence of either unique identification or chain of custody. Authentication of real evidence satisfies our concerns about whether the item under consideration is the actual item in question and that it was not altered or tampered with in any material way. The police officer's initials scratched in the grip of the gun at the time it was taken from the murder suspect allow the officer to identify the gun as the right one, distinguishing it from all other guns of the same manufacturer and model; an initialed seal on the contaminated bottle of champagne may mark it sufficiently to permit it to be introduced in the food-poisoning trial. Items that cannot be so marked—like crystalline, white powder—must instead be carefully tracked through a chain of observation and possession—a chain of custody—so that some sequence of witnesses can testify that they had control of, or sight of, the item continuously from the time it gained relevance to the time—perhaps after some final test on it by the defense or perhaps at trial—at which its physical integrity becomes unimportant.

For example, the white powder taken from the street dealer is placed in a plastic bag, sealed, initialed, and locked in the officer's cruiser. It is then placed in the evidence lockup and later signed out to the chemical laboratory. The lab technician opens the sample and conducts the tests, recording the results that show that the powder is cocaine. The technician seals and marks the remainder so that the defense can be given an opportunity to test the same sample. To connect the powder from the defendant's pocket to the test results presented in court, the prosecutor brings in the police officer, the evidence lockup custodian, and the lab technician, each of whom testifies to the state of the evidence at the time they handled it. (In reality, the police officer may be able to provide sufficient evidence of the regularity and reliability of the evidence lockup that the custodian will not be needed; instead, the court will accept the officer's statement that he signed it in and was the only one to sign it out.)[3] The chain of custody is the sequential presentation of evidence of unique identification; that is, the police officer can uniquely identify the powder because he kept control of it; the lab technician has the same ability to uniquely identify it. Each witness provides a link in the chain of custody by showing a period of control or continuous observation of the item of evidence. The gun is uniquely identified in court as the relevant gun by the officer's initials carved in the grip. It could also be identified as the relevant gun by showing the links in the chain of custody—that it was under continuous observation and could not have been subjected to tampering in any relevant way.[4]

---

3. In criminal cases, because of the Constitutional requirement of confrontation deriving from the Sixth Amendment, the government may be limited in its ability to satisfy chain of custody requirements through the use of substitutes for testimony, like certifications from officials.

4. In many instances, modern rules allow declarations to provide the necessary link; see, e.g., FED. R. EVID. 902(4) and (12).

National Institute for Trial Advocacy

2.10 Limit of Chain of Custody

The chain of custody need only extend to the point in time at which relevance ends. In the example given above of the white powder taken from the suspect, it is necessary to track the custody and treatment of the powder from the time it is taken from the suspect to the time it is tested by the lab technician (or, perhaps, to the time it is delivered for testing to the defendant's expert). After the laboratory tests are completed and the results are recorded, there is no particular need to be concerned with the possibility of tampering or alteration. Therefore, the chain needs to extend only from the frisk and seizure to the completion of the lab test. If, on the other hand, the actual exhibit is going to be used in a substantive demonstration in court—such as showing that there is contamination in the champagne bottle—then the chain of custody must extend to the time of presentation in court.

2.11 Keep Counsel Out of Chain of Custody

You, as the attorney, should not become a link in the chain of custody. Until the end of the relevant period for the integrity of the item of evidence, do not take possession of evidence that can be altered. For example, with the contaminated champagne discussed in the previous paragraph, if you want to show the contamination in court, the relevant period for the integrity of the evidence does not end until the bottle and its contents are shown in court. Therefore, do not take the bottle from the witness outside of the courtroom and then hand it up to the witness on the stand for identification, unless the bottle has been sealed in some unique way that the witness can discuss. If the bottle has been in your possession, then its integrity depends in part on your observation and custody. Since you normally will not be allowed to testify on such a substantive matter, the chain of custody has been broken, and the foundation may be inadequate.

2.12 Substantive, Demonstrative, and Illustrative Evidence

Substantive evidence is evidence on which a jury may base its findings and verdict. One category of evidence, demonstrative evidence, has intrinsic substantive value and therefore may be the basis for findings of fact. Another category of evidence, illustrative evidence, is not substantive and merely helps to explain the witness's testimony. It cannot be the basis for findings or a verdict.

2.13   Demonstrative Evidence

As opposed to merely illustrative evidence, the results of a demonstration are intended to have evidentiary significance. For example, jurors may rely on an admissible demonstration in which sparks from an electrical short circuit ignite vapors from jet fuel as the jurors come to conclusions about causation, regardless of whether there is accompanying testimony. Demonstrative exhibits normally have independent substantive value (as, for example, a demonstration of the effect of mixing two chemicals provides information to the trier-of-fact, which may be used to support findings), even though the demonstrative exhibits may also *illustrate* points made in the witness's testimony. Substantive exhibits obviously have substantive value—that is, they can provide support to findings of fact; they may perhaps be demonstrative, but they are never merely illustrative.

2.14 Illustrative Evidence

Exhibits that are intended merely to illustrate a witness's testimony are admissible to the extent that the testimony is. They have no independent substantive value. Further, if a witness presents an exhibit to show what he is talking about, like a graph or sketch or diagram, and his testimony is then excluded or rejected, the illustrative exhibit will likewise be excluded or rejected. An illustration on the whiteboard of the appearance of the intersection at the moment of the collision, sketched by the witness without any claim that it is to scale or is otherwise accurate and introduced to help the jurors understand the witness's testimony, is illustrative only. It has no life beyond that witness's testimony, and it will not survive if the testimony is stricken for some reason. Illustrative exhibits have no substantive probative value of their own, but derive their probative value entirely from the testimony they illustrate. (When an expert's testimony is stricken or limited for some reason, illustrations of the points she was trying to make should also be stricken.)

Chapter Three

Common Problems with Graphic Exhibits

3.1 Comparison Exhibits

To persuasively emphasize changed conditions, use a graphic that shows before and after views simultaneously or prepare two exhibits that can be presented side-by-side. Comparisons—such as differences over time, growth, or response to variables—are much more effective when presented in a graphic exhibit that displays the two conditions simultaneously. If the changes are displayed in a series of graphics, the jurors do not see them simultaneously, and so they must rely on their memories to track the changes in the quantity and even location (from 1,573 to 1,945; this row, that column; that door, this window; or right lung, lower lobe). Instead, display the before and after (or healthy and sick, or unmodified and modified) views on the same graphic, at the same time, side-by-side, with the differences colored or highlighted or circled (perhaps by the witness with a magic marker) so that they appear clearly.

3.2 Misleading Icons

Look for misleading icons not only in your opponent's graphics, but your own, as well. Misleading icons are symbols that unfairly exaggerate relevant information in a graphic. They are therefore cause for the court to reject the exhibit. For example, doubling the height and width of a bar in a bar chart to show that the quantity has doubled since the previous month actually quadruples the visual area. If the chart is drawn in three dimensions and each dimension (height, width, and length) is doubled, the visual impact (now not area, but volume) is multiplied eightfold. The visual impact, especially if the error continues with further increases (what if, in the third month, the quantity "doubles again?), can be enormously misleading.

3.3 Misleading Labels

Similarly, look for misleading labels in both your graphics and your opponent's. Misleading labels can exaggerate the extent of change or difference. As an example, a graph purporting to show yearly sales volumes (and perhaps even entitled, "Yearly Sales Volumes") is misleading if the last amount shown is for less than a year (a problem that can be thought of as an "apple-orange problem," because you are comparing full periods to partial periods).

On a much more subtle level, a bar graph showing growth in profits from $10 million to $13 million, with the baseline at $0, will show the second bar as 1.3 times as high as the first; but if the baseline is labeled to begin at $9 million, the first bar will be one unit high (showing $1 million over the baseline) and the second bar will be four units high, or four times the height of the first.

3.4 Exclusion of Misleading Exhibits

Graphics that are misleading because of icon, label, axis/baseline, "apple-orange," or other problems are likely to be excluded under Rule 403.

Once a proper objection is made, misleading graphics will be rejected until they are corrected; therefore, if the error is not discovered or disclosed until trial, you may have no opportunity to prepare a fair graphic exhibit and you may lose the evidence. Of course, if there is some reason to believe that an honest error was known, but the objection was withheld intentionally, the court might find waiver of the objection, permitting the exhibit to be corrected even during trial.

3.5 Visual Impact

Graphic exhibits must have *immediate visual impact* to be effective. Experiment with different displays, changing variables and axes, until the exhibit shows emphasis and message you want. Graphics containing information about several factors often may not provide sufficient emphasis to the data on the particular variable that is most important: a chart showing blood pressure, white cell count, and respiration may make blood pressure disappear into the forest, even though it could be the most important factor. Simplify the display by eliminating variables that are less relevant or explanatory.

Try different colors (or a single color for the important data while other data is in black and white). Do not be satisfied with the exhibit until a lay person, looking at it for the first time, is able to state the point you want to make with the data you are relying on. Ask secretaries and other nonlawyers in the office; ask neighbors and friends. When you are opposing graphic evidence, look for changes in scale or perspective that might exaggerate or unduly emphasize the point being made. Be especially wary of a plan (overhead) view or a grid-type three-dimensional picture of a scene. These can be tilted so that jurors will see some things more easily than any witness ever saw them. For example, the depiction may present a bird's-eye view, which no one had, suggesting that the defendant saw all the danger points simultaneously and without obstruction or distraction.

When opposing graphic evidence, look carefully at the labels on those exhibits and consider the appropriateness of the label to the use of the exhibit at trial. Are the labels argumentative? Should they therefore be excluded from opening statement? Do the labels lead? Should they be excluded from direct examination? Do the labels mischaracterize evidence? Should they therefore be excluded completely? Do the labels misstate what was received in evidence? Should they therefore be excluded from closing?

3.6 Graphic Evidence v. Enlargements

Do not mistake "big text documents" for "graphic evidence." A "blow-up" of a document, especially of a text document, is merely a big text document—it does not tell a story visually. Pictures, charts, graphs, videos, or computer animations make effective visual exhibits if they produce an immediate reaction in the viewer that supports the theme of your case. To cite an extreme example, an accounting worksheet or table, filled with rows and columns of numbers, has little visual impact (unless the theme is boredom); but, if the numbers are all written in gray, with just the final number in the far right column, bottom row written as **($22,183,047)**, then the viewer's immediate reaction to the exhibit is that somebody lost a lot of money. Having isolated the elements needed to promote visual impact, you should then ask why the other elements are necessary at all—all those other rows and columns of numbers have become nothing more than background. Perhaps they should be dimmed, like the computer programs do with commands that are unavailable at a particular time.

3.7 Trimming Irrelevant Detail

Do not lose relevant points among irrelevant details. Even enlarged picture exhibits are not effective if the relevant details are lost among other items in the scene. By direct analogy to the accounting worksheet discussed above, a pictorial scene may contain the relevant information, but not display it effectively because of the clutter caused by other items in the scene. To avoid any charges of unfairness or tampering, present the enlarged picture without enhancement, and then present alongside the original an enhancement in which the relevant item is circled and the remainder dimmed. TV sportscasts are highlighting the player being discussed in a circle of light, like a spotlight. You could also circle the relevant item and "call it out" with an arrow leading to an enlargement of that section off in the margin, or in some other way draw attention to the important component and leave the remainder as background. Otherwise, you could just as well hand small versions of the visual exhibit to each juror for his close inspection. The advantage of visual exhibits is that they provide the opportunity to emphasize particular information through the eyes of the viewer.

3.8 Marking or Editing an Exhibit

In most courts, neither you nor any of your witnesses may alter, mark or edit an opponent's graphic once it has been received in evidence. You may, however, make your own copy and mark it or overlay your opponent's original with an acetate sheet and have your witness or the opponent's witness mark the sheet. You may then offer the marked copy or graphic in evidence. Assuming that the markings are relevant, the marked-up copy is just as admissible as the testimony and the original exhibit, and it should be considered by the judge or jury along with that original under Rule 106. There is little satisfaction greater than turning an opponent's graphic evidence against him by pointing out errors or inconsistencies or by highlighting portions that support your case, especially if you can enlist the opponent's witness in the effort.

Chapter Four

Handling Documents in Court

4.1 Marking an Exhibit

When you are ready to offer an exhibit in court, let the judge know what you want to do. If the documents have been premarked, as is the case in most courts, there is no need to separately get the court reporter to mark a document. During your witness examination or otherwise, stand and tell the judge, "Your Honor, may I give the witness (or, "May I ask the clerk to give the witness . . .") a document that has been premarked for identification as Exhibit 7."

4.2 The Three-Step Exhibit Circuit

Make the "three-step exhibit circuit" when presenting an item of evidence at trial. Carry three copies of the exhibit with you, and place one copy on opposing counsel's table, saying, "Counsel" audibly, so that it is apparent to all that you have provided a copy. Next, say, "Your Honor, would you like a copy?" And third, hand the witness a copy, saying, "Mr. Hobart, I'm handing you what has been marked as Plaintiff's Exhibit 7 for identification."

The first step prevents opposing counsel from interrupting your examination about the exhibit by asking for a copy or by insisting on a comparison of his copy with the one the witness is using. The second step makes certain that the judge is following the examination with her copy of the document; if the judge has her copy, she'll say, "Thank you." That's nice. If the judge does not have her copy, she will take one from you, and say, "Thank you." That's nice, too. The third step makes it clear in the record that the witness has a copy of the exhibit in front of him so you do not need to make any artificial statements, such as, "Your Honor, I would like the record to reflect that I am handing the witness . . . ."

4.3 Laying the Foundation

Lay the foundation for the exhibit and offer it in evidence before asking questions about its

contents and substance. Until the court has ruled
on whether there is a proper basis for admitting
the exhibit in evidence, its substance and content
should not be put into the record or discussed in
front of the jury. Of course, with some exhibits,
you will need to refer to the contents, in a limited way, to identify the contents as relevant. For
example, the foundation for a photograph of the
accident scene consists of some witness identifying
the photograph as a fair and accurate depiction of
the relevant scene at a relevant time. Testimony on
the contents beyond that would be inappropriate,
however, until the exhibit is received, so before it
is, you should not ask the witness, "Is that how
the plaintiff's body looked as it protruded through
the windshield of the defendant's truck?" And you
should object if your opponent tries to do so with
her exhibit.

4.4 Offering the Exhibit

After you have completed the foundation for
the exhibit, say, "Your Honor, I offer Plaintiff's
Exhibit 13 in evidence." Nothing more complex
is required. It is not necessary to say, "Your Honor,
we would like to move the admission of Plaintiff's

Exhibit 13," or anything to that effect. The simple "I offer" is sufficient. Counsel sometimes say, "I offer Plaintiff's Exhibit 13 for identification in evidence and ask that the identifying mark be stricken," but, because there is no real possibility of ambiguity as to what is happening, this excess and archaic verbiage should be omitted.

4.5 Distributing the Exhibit

Do not distract jurors by distributing documents during important testimony. Distribute the jurors' copies of a complicated exhibit after they hear the testimony about the exhibit. If they receive their copies too early, they will busy themselves with reviewing them and miss portions of the testimony. If the testimony about an exhibit will take a few minutes, as when there are several portions of the exhibit to discuss, hold the jurors' copies until the testimony is completed and ask them to watch the overhead or blow-up while they listen to the testimony. Of course, if you want the jurors to take notes on their copies of the exhibit, you could distribute the copies before the testimony and then emphasize the notable portions in the testimony.

4.6   Offering for a Limited Purpose

If the offer in evidence is not explicitly limited, then it is general. There are times when an exhibit is offered for a limited purpose, such as showing that a statement has been made, regardless of its truth, thereby avoiding a hearsay objection ("And is that the article in which he called you a cheating and conniving liar?", offered for the limited purpose of proving that the libel was made and not to prove that the witness is in fact a cheating and conniving liar."). If that is your purpose, you should say, "Your Honor, we offer Plaintiff's Exhibit 13 in evidence for the limited purpose of showing that the defendant made the allegedly defamatory statement." When such a limited offer is made, the jury will normally be instructed that they are to consider the exhibit only to show that the statement was made, and not for the truth of the statement itself. A limited offer might also be made where the evidence is offered against one codefendant or against fewer than all of the members of a class.

4.7   Publishing the Exhibit

When "publishing" exhibits, that is, when showing them to the jurors, consider the advantages and disadvantages of three different display options: camera-to-screen; computer-to-screen; and computer/DVR-to-monitor.

4.7.1 Camera to Screen

The evidence camera-to-screen option is the most versatile display option and the easiest to operate. It requires only that you know how to turn on the camera's power button, place the exhibit (document, picture, or object) under the lens, focus, and then move the exhibit to show what you want to show. The camera will then show a picture of the exhibit on a display screen. You can zoom for details. This method provides excellent backup in case other media fail.

4.7.2 Computer to Screen

A second option is the computer-to-screen configuration. Many courtrooms today have projection systems that will display images from computer programs (PowerPoint, Summation, etc.) onto a screen. PowerPoint, Corel Presentations, and other presentation software can access slides or files containing exhibits, pictures, and videos at the scanning of a bar code or the push of a button.

A separate foundation for the exhibit shown on the screen does not need to be laid. Once the proponent has laid the foundation of the exhibit with a copy and the witness, offered the exhibit, and had it received, then the proponent, as an officer of the court, can simply ask that the technician show the exhibit to the jury. The exhibit is then projected for everyone to see. You must take care to insure that the details and the lettering are large enough for the jurors and court to see. The following formula may be useful in determining whether an audience will be able to read text on the screen: $D/20 = H$, where D is the distance in feet to the most distant person, and H is the height in inches of the letters or symbol on the exhibit that must be seen.

4.7.3 Computer/DVR to Monitor

A third option is computer/DVR to monitor. Depending on the number and size of monitors in the courtroom, this may be the best approach: sound quality can be excellent, and by using the monitors, you remind the audience of their home television news shows. If the judge and witness have monitors, you can lay the foundation without premature disclosure to the jury. After the exhibit is received in evidence, the court would push a button and the jurors' screens would be activated.

4.7.4 Other Tips for Visual Presentations

Whatever option you choose, remember these ten tips for visual presentations:

1. If you display a picture, show one per slide or board and have no more than seven words on it.

2. Use professional colors and graphic devices, like boxes and borders.

3. Avoid overly slick displays.

4. Do not talk to the visual on the screen or easel; talk to the trier-of-fact, then point out something additional on the graphic, then turn back to the audience to discuss it.

5. Stand alongside the visual and face the audience.

6. Do not show the visual until you have introduced the topic with one or two sentences from the witness.

7. Point to relevant portions as you speak or reveal points as they come up.

8. Remember the "three Ts: touch, turn, and talk," and, on direct, have the witness do the touching, turning, and talking about the exhibit.

9. Do not talk and write simultaneously on flip charts or pads.

10. Pause for emphasis, turn your back and write without speaking, then turn back, reestablish eye contact, and reveal what you have written. Teach your witness to follow this process.

4.8 Ordering Exhibits

Present your exhibits (and your overall story) in chronological order, if possible, at least within a topic. The exceptions to this approach may overwhelm the rule; nevertheless, your first approach to organizing the story, and the exhibits accompanying the story, should be chronological. In preparation, first chart out the story; then arrange the witnesses to cover the time period of the story (with overlapping coverage); then rearrange the witnesses after determining their availability; and finally arrange the exhibits, first chronologically and then distributed among the witnesses as necessary so foundations can be laid. Some courts require that the exhibits be numbered in the order in which they are offered at trial; the only practical way to do that is to number them as they are offered (and have your back-up help number the copies for opposing counsel and your files simultaneously). If the documents are pre-numbered and then introduced out of numerical order, find some opportunity, in opening or when the first document is admitted, to explain to the jury that the numbers have nothing to do with the importance of the document. Explain that the numbers are just a way to keep track of sheets of paper and other items, and the jurors should not be concerned about the number sequence.

4.9 Jurors' Notebooks

Jurors' notebooks, where allowed, should contain your *important* documents, not *all* your documents. If the fourteen documents that win your case are buried among 312 other documents, the jurors will not give them proper attention; in other words, the impact of the most important documents will be diluted by the presence of the other documents.[1] During your opening statement, tell the jurors that you will give them copies of the most important documents for them to place in their own notebooks; then, when you do give them a document, it will come with your implicit "certificate of importance." If, at the end of the trial, your fourteen documents are aligned against your opponent's 312, you can argue that your opponent has tried to confuse the issues and the evidence and has cluttered the record with irrelevant documents and testimony. If, however, the court insists that all documents be placed in the jurors' notebooks, ask your witness the following questions on the stand, as appropriate: "Which of these three documents was most important to you in deciding to enter this contract?" "Which of these photographs did you find most useful in understanding the causes of the fire?" "Which of these charts provides the best summary of the performance of this industry during the 1990s?"

---

1. *See infra* Rule J.6 for the fourteen document rule.

Then, in closing, you can recall that testimony for the jury and invite them to take note of those more important documents.

4.10 Sightlines

Consider the sightlines in the courtroom when you are presenting visual evidence. It is very frustrating for a juror or judge to be presented with a chart, document, or photograph that is too far away, on too much of an angle to read easily, or obscured by a glare from the window. Before the trial, check out the courtroom sightlines several times during the day, so you can see how the light changes. Put a colleague in the jury box and another on the witness stand to determine where to place the easel or screen to allow clear viewing. You should not block your opponent's sightlines of the exhibits or put the jury or the witness behind the exhibits. If there is no reasonable way to arrange the exhibits without blocking the opponent, you should explain that to the court and ask the court's permission to locate the exhibit so the jury and witness can see it, with the opposing counsel being invited to move around to the front of the exhibit to view the examination. You want the judge to see the exhibit, also, but reasonable judges understand that the witness and the jurors come first in this stage management. If you cannot work out an arrangement in which the judge can see the exhibit from her bench, then explain that to the judge and provide the judge with an additional copy of the exhibit, perhaps larger than previous copies, so the court can follow the examination. Of course, if the witness is doing something to the exhibit, then your choreography must allow the judge to observe the testimony. Using video cameras mounted vertically and aimed downward to capture and then present an image of a document or item onto a large screen, sometimes called "document cameras" or "Elmos," make this determination of sightlines much easier.

CHAPTER FIVE

CHOOSING THE MEDIUM AND THE OCCASION

5.1 Using Exhibits in Opening Statement

An exhibit can be used in opening statement if you have a good-faith basis for believing it is admissible. In a small minority of jurisdictions, using an exhibit in opening statement is forbidden, apparently on the theory that the jury should not be exposed to material that has not yet been admitted into the record (although some jurisdictions within this small minority even prohibit using exhibits in the opening statement that were admitted pretrial, on an unknown rationale). Certainly, during the presentation of evidence, exhibits are not shown to the jury until they are offered and received in evidence. However, testimony is routinely referred to in openings, even though no witness has yet taken the stand. If the opening is indeed supposed to present a preview of the evidence, that preview should logically include the documentary and physical evidence as well. If there is visual evidence that presents a serious danger of unfair prejudice, that problem could be considered on motion in limine, and the court could admit or reject it at that time, or it could reserve a ruling until the foundation is heard at trial and direct that the particular exhibit not be used in the opening statement.

5.2 Using Exhibits in Closing Argument

In closing argument, review the *important* visual and documentary exhibits, not *all* the exhibits. You must avoid overwhelming the jurors, especially after they have just sat through both your and your opponent's presentations of the entire case. Once again, select the exhibits that make a difference, just as you select certain testimony to emphasize. Where you used a series of exhibits at trial (for example, to show growth, change, or other comparisons), consider whether you could present the first and last exhibits in the series, to help the jury remember the scope of the change or difference. Remember to find out whether in your jurisdiction merely illustrative exhibits are excluded from the jury room (as the transcribed testimony they illustrate is excluded); if you highlight those illustrative exhibits in your closing, the jurors could be disappointed or confused when the illustrative exhibits are not available to them during deliberations.

With PowerPoint, Corel Presentations, or similar programs, remember that less is more. The lure of the technology of presentations software is seductive, because it is both fun to create shows and fun to share your notes with the audience. Yet you need to stay in touch with your audience and the nonverbal clues the audience members provide about their interest and skepticism. If you are too wedded to your prepared presentations, you will likely lose the jurors' attention. Furthermore, the power of the screen means that the jurors may stop paying attention to you and instead watch the screen. Remember that they need time to read the screen, so avoid speaking over their reading. To avoid both the competition with the screen and the boredom of too many slides, mix your medium. Start by talking to the jury directly, then use timelines and charts, then introduce a few slides of your most important documents and pictures, with callouts. Then, for the last portion of your closing, turn the technology off, look the jurors in their eyes, and talk directly to them. With technology and closing, less is more.

5.3 Timelines

Timelines are essential exhibits. Events happen in the flow of time—chronologically—and often can be understood only against a background of a timeline. Timelines are not vertical lists of events arranged by date; they are horizontal calendar-bars into which events have been asserted. If you present a timeline exhibit to the jurors early in the case, they will be able to follow the flow of events more easily and understand the facts more clearly. If your version of events depends on showing confusion, disorganization, or lack of coordination—such as where you are trying to show absence of conspiracy or plan in defending a RICO case or a failure to respond appropriately to an emergency in prosecuting a personal injury case—then your goal would be to display many events on a timeline, emphasizing the lack of chronological relevance among them. A timeline exhibit created in front of the jurors, event by event, in a sense invites their participation; as a result, they become invested in the exhibit and protective of it, resisting and resenting efforts by opposing counsel to dismiss it or to change it without sufficient basis.

5.4 Magnetism

Choose your medium to entertain and organize. "It's magnetism!" they shouted, "Magnetism!" Magnetic cards that stick to a lightweight, steel-backed whiteboard are a very effective way to present thematic words, category titles, and essential quotes. The process of adding, subtracting, and rearranging words and phrases on a magnetic whiteboard is neat, quick, and simple. You can emphasize the subject of particular testimony, give a heading to a listing of factors, or add a picture to a speaker's words without distracting from your own performance by relying on your own poor public penmanship. You can also color code the magnetic cards, so related ideas are immediately associated with one another.

5.5 Multiple Easels

Use multiple easels to display different exhibits simultaneously. There are times when you need to show two boards so the jurors can appreciate the difference or the progression. In fact, putting a visual exhibit on easel A, then a different one on B, then a new one on A, and so on, keeps the show moving forward while allowing the audience (judge or jury) to see where it has been. If a computer graphic is projected on a screen between the two easels, then a little coordination results in a multi-media tour de force (although there is some serious danger of distraction and confusion to be avoided here).

5.6 Monitors v. Big Screen

Television or computer monitors are sometimes more effective than big screen projection; but sometimes they are not. Jury analysts report that jurors tend to believe what they see on television because of their association of television with Edward R. Murrow, Walter Cronkite, Tim Russert, Brian Williams, and other trusted commentators. In contrast, big screens are often associated with "Star Wars," "Harry Potter," and other dramatic fictions. Another reason to use monitors is that they can be seen in normal lighting. Television is, however, ubiquitous in jurors' homes and has become part of the background noise, while big-screen movies promise excitement and entertainment. So, here is a guide to choosing among static boards, displays on monitors, and projections on a big screen:

1. If motion is not important to the point being made, use boards on easels;

2. If the segment depends on motion, like a deposition or demonstration, and it is short, use the monitors, because they are bright, easy-on and -off, and very reliable; and

3. If the exhibit needs motion, but is longer, use the big-screen projection so any background distractions are reduced and the main points can be clearly seen.

Remember, with any of these presentation modes, the material must be high-interest; otherwise, the jury would prefer to see live cross-examination, experts defending their opinions to the death, and battles between real flesh-and-blood lawyers who succeed by their wits, just like on "Harry's Law," "Law and Order," and "The Good Wife."

5.7 Cards

Hold magnetic or velcro cards, or small items of real evidence, while you ask questions about them. The jurors look from you to the witness and back while they listen to the questions and answers. You present a memorable picture if you are holding a foamboard card that reads, "Nicotine is addictive," while you question the expert about label warnings; or a card that reads, "No reliable studies," while you cross-examine on bases for expert testimony; or a piece of rusted metal from the actual building while you ask the architect questions about the adequacy of corrosion protection of the steel embedded in the foundation. In other words, do something with your visual or physical evidence in addition to putting it in front of the jurors' eyes. Talk about it. Walk with it. Handle it. Hand it to your witness as he steps from the witness box and ask him to put it up on the magnetic board or to hold it in the same position it had in the building. Then, when that line of questioning is finished, and you ask the court for two minutes to check your notes, ask if the document or item of real evidence can be passed to the jurors for their examination. (If the document is not already in their notebooks, this is the time to pass out copies so as not to interrupt your examination.)

5.8   Do Not "Publish"

Do not ask to "publish" admitted documents to the jury; ask instead to be allowed to show or hand the document or piece of evidence to the jurors. Each time you use specialized language or archaic legal terms, you remind the jurors that you are a lawyer, and they are not. Since your goal is to communicate, to relate, and to teach, use familiar language, not language that requires constant interpretation and translation.

Chapter Six

Experts and Exhibits

6.1 Disclosures

Under Federal Rule of Civil Procedure 26, you must voluntarily disclose all exhibits the testifying expert will use. This mandatory "voluntary" disclosure includes documents, data compilations, and tangible things;[1] documents underlying damage computations;[2] insurance agreements;[3] and, beyond trial exhibits, an expert report and exhibits to be used by the expert."[4]

The nonexpert disclosures must be made not more than ten days after the Rule 26(f) meeting,

---

1. FED. R. CIV. P. 26(a)(1)(B).
2. FED. R. CIV. P. 26(a)(1)(C).
3. FED. R. CIV. P. 26(a)(1)(D).
4. FED. R. CIV. P. 26(a)(2)(B).

which itself must be held at least fourteen days
before a scheduling conference or the date for a
scheduling order. Therefore, determine the date
set for the scheduling conference; count back
fourteen days (including intervening Saturdays,
Sundays, and legal holidays), then count forward ten days (apparently excluding intervening
Saturdays, Sundays, and legal holidays). (Because
of the time computation provisions of Rule 8, the
"fourteen back, ten forward" count could actually
result in the ten-day period expiring after the
scheduling conference, but parties can avoid this
unintended result by agreement or court direc-
tion.) That date is the latest date for the disclosure
of the Rule 26 documents and other materials.
The expert disclosures and report-in-chief must be
submitted ninety days before trial for the report-
in-chief and related materials; a rebuttal report, if
prepared, must be submitted thirty days after the
report which it is rebutting.[5]

At least thirty days before trial, the parties must
identify the documents they intend to offer and
must separately identify the documents they may

---

5. FED. R. CIV. P. 26(a)(2)(D).

offer, excluding documents they intend to use solely for impeachment purposes. Objections (other than relevance or unfair prejudice) to an opponent's documents must be made within fourteen days of this identification or they are deemed waived.[6]

6.2 Persuasive Exhibits

Persuasive exhibits make expert testimony more credible and understandable. The premise of expert testimony is that it presents information to the jurors that is beyond their ken. They need the help of an expert to understand a process like the conversion of gasoline into energy to move a car; or to understand a relationship like that between a tainted vaccine and the disease it causes; or a phenomenon like an avalanche in the Rocky Mountains. The jurors must find the expert to be credible and must understand at least the structure of the methodology the expert has employed; then they can rely on the expert's testimony. The jurors do not have to be trained to the point that they can independently replicate the expert's studies, experiments, or clinical

---

6. FED. R. CIV. P. 26(a)(3).

investigations, but the expert testimony cannot remain "charming but incomprehensible," as the painter Edgar Degas characterized the "conversation of specialists." Therefore, the expert's exhibits must be especially helpful, especially interesting, and especially memorable.

6.3 Theme

The essential portions of the expert's Rule 26(b) report should provide the themes for the expert's illustrative or summary visual exhibits. The expert's report often contains more information than the jury needs to remember because it is intended 1) to reveal all of the expert's bases and opinions, 2) to serve as a vehicle for pretrial discovery, and 3) to provide a basis for the court's rulings on admissibility of the expert's testimony under *Daubert* and *Kumho Tire*. Nevertheless, you can identify the most important opinions in the report and use those as the basis for interesting trial exhibits. An outline of the report will provide a list of its most important points; from that list, you can probably identify five opinions and bases that justify interesting graphic exhibits of their own. If this outline approach does not suggest effective exhibits, create a new list of high-level opinions with the expert and brainstorm on ways to visualize them. (Make certain, of course, that these opinions are contained within the Rule 26(b) report provided to your opponent.)

6.4 Foundation for Illustrative Exhibits

The foundation for an expert's illustrative exhibits is that the exhibit will help the expert give testimony. When you reach the appropriate point in the expert's direct examination, plan to ask the expert, "Have you prepared any exhibits to help you explain this to us?" (Notice that the phrase is, "to us," not "to the jury." Do not separate yourself from the jurors or suggest that you are well-informed and they are ill-informed, by asking, "Can you explain this to the jury?") For variety, you may also ask, "Can you show us what you mean?" or "Is there some way we can see that?" or any other question that cues your expert that it's time for a picture show.

6.5 Work the Exhibits

During direct examination, bring your expert off the stand so she can work with visual exhibits.

Getting the expert out of the witness box allows her to move around, talk with more animation, and teach the jurors more naturally. So use the visual exhibits to get the expert witness to come down and interact. Say, "Your Honor, may the witness come down to use an exhibit on the easel (or projector) to explain this point?" Schedule exhibits for times when the jurors' (or judge's) attention and energy may be low: midmorning before the break, right before lunch, four o'clock in the afternoon.

6.6 Keep Opposing Expert on the Stand

During cross-examination, keep the opposing expert in her seat and resist her attempts to get in front of the jurors with an exhibit. On cross-examination, watch for attempts by the well-prepared opposing expert to maneuver you into letting her come down and explain something with visual exhibits. Beware the opposing expert who says on cross-examination, "Well, counsel, if I could just come down and show you what I mean on an exhibit I used earlier," or "Counsel, it might help the jury and judge if I just showed them a diagram that I have in my exhibit case." Respond to those requests with something like, "Let's just talk about this point for a moment, and then we can decide if we need the exhibit," or "Let me ask something else here, and then perhaps we'll come back to that area if we have time." Of course, whether you actually do come back to that area later is up to you.

6.7 Attacking the Exhibit

Experts' exhibits can be attacked with the same tools used to attack expert testimony. As presented elsewhere,[7] expert testimony can often be attacked by identifying things the expert did *not* do, information the expert did *not* consider, and assumptions the expert had to make. To the extent the expert's exhibits reflect or illustrate the opinions that suffer from these same weaknesses, they may be turned to the advantage of the cross-examiner. For example, if the expert has calculated the present value of a future income stream, which requires that assumptions be made about future interest rates and inflation rates, an exhibit showing that calculation

---

7. David Malone, Paul Zwier, Expert Rules, 3d ed. (NITA 2012).

embodies whatever assumptions the expert made about those variables. Using the expert's deposition testimony on the range of assumptions that were reasonable and the same computerized formula that generated the expert's results shown on the chart, first have the expert "guide" you through duplicating her result (displaying it side-by-side with the expert's own chart to show that they are identical); then have the expert help you enter your chosen, reasonable alternative assumptions. Display the resulting chart alongside the expert's own chart so the jury can compare them. To finish such a line of cross-examination, present a third chart showing the alternative assumptions next to the different results (e.g., the expert's 4.7 percent next to his $2 million, and your alternative 5.5 percent next to your $43.18 million). Use the opposing expert to lay the foundation for each of these additional exhibits, which are merely variations on his own, by leading him through the appropriate testimony. During such examination, you must emphasize through repetition that you and the expert are following the same methodology he followed when he created his original exhibit.

6.8 Creating New Exhibits during Cross-Examination

If you create a new exhibit during expert cross-examination, number it and offer it in evidence. It may be illustrative if it has no intrinsic substantive value, but merely illustrates the expert's testimony (or your cross-examination); or it may be substantive if the expert has allowed you to lay the foundation for new substantive information contained or displayed in the exhibit (like the "new" answers obtained from alternative assumptions or perhaps from a learned treatise that you have used pursuant to Federal Rule of Evidence 803(18)). Regardless of its evidentiary status, have the exhibit numbered and admitted, even if it is for a limited purpose, so you can refer to it during later examinations and closing argument.

6.9 Counter Opposing Counsel's Attempt to Create New Cross Exhibits

Give your own expert the ammunition to counter opposing counsel's attempts to create new "cross-examination exhibits." During preparation for testimony at trial, remember to tell your expert that opposing counsel may try to create new exhibits or alter the expert's own exhibits. Tell your expert that when it is true, he can disagree with the cross-examiner's new exhibits by saying, "That's not my methodology, but I can explain further," or "That's not what I did, but I will be happy to show you my approach." The cross-examiner must rely on a hostile expert to lay the foundation for the new exhibit. Therefore, your expert should understand that when it is the truth, he can say, "I think that your new exhibit is misleading," and the court may not receive the exhibit or the jury may not give it any weight. Of course, you need to make sure the expert knows that there are trigger words, like "misleading," "incomplete," or "confusing," that are more effective than others in frustrating such cross-examination on revised exhibits.

CHAPTER SEVEN

EVIDENTIARY PRINCIPLES FOR CERTAIN TYPES OF DOCUMENTS

7.1 Foundation Formulas

Learn the foundational formulas for the most frequently encountered exhibit situations. As noted in the first section of this book, "OPRAH" (Original document rule, Privilege, Relevance, Authenticity, and Hearsay) captures all of the foundational elements necessary for the analysis of any evidentiary problem. The law at its roots is a search for peaceful solutions among problems previously solved. The area of evidentiary foundations presents recurring exhibit problems for which past solutions can be identified and used again and again.

7.2 Business Records

Business records must be shown to have been created in the ordinary course of the business or activity, as a matter of routine, to avoid exclusion as hearsay. Under Rule 803(6), the "record of regularly conducted activity" or "business record" exception to the rule excluding hearsay, out-of-court statements prepared in the routine course of a business, not in anticipation of litigation, may be received in evidence even though they are classic hearsay because of the trustworthiness associated with the routine nature of their creation. The great majority of documents in business cases are from the files of the businesses involved. Although documents created by the opposing party are party statements or admissions under Rule 801(d), and therefore non-hearsay in the federal system or an exception to the rule excluding hearsay in many state systems, documents from your own client's files are hearsay unless an exception, usually the business records exception, is shown to apply. In your foundation questioning, concentrate on the facts that show that:

- the documents were created before the litigation;

- the documents were created, used, and kept in the day-to-day operation of the business;

- by a person with knowledge of the events recorded.

7.3 Past Recollection

Documents containing past recollection may be received, but they must be read to the jury and not admitted as paper documents into the record like other exhibits. Under Rule 803(5), out-of-court statements that constitute past recollection recorded are admissible if the witness's present memory has failed or been exhausted and the document can be shown to have been created near the time of the events recorded. Part of the foundation for past recollection recorded is a demonstration that the witness's present recollection cannot be refreshed. If your witness has indicated that he is having difficulty remembering ("I guess that's about all I know on that"), ask directly, "Do you remember who else was in the meeting?" If the witness says, "No," the stage is set for completing the foundation for introducing the contents of the document as "past recollection recorded" with the use of the exhibit containing past recollection.

- Provide a copy of the exhibit to opposing counsel, the court, and the witness, and have the witness identify the document containing the past recollection.

- Take the document back and ask the witness, "Having looked at Exhibit 14, can you now recall who else was at the meeting."

- This time, when the witness says, "No," you are ready to introduce the exhibit as past recollection recorded.

- Say: "Tell us the circumstances in which this document, Exhibit 14 for identification, was created."

- In your foundation questioning, emphasize the nonlitigation purpose for which the record was created. This helps satisfy your burden that that the document is trustworthy, even though it was created out-of-court on an occasion when the adversary could not cross-examine the writer.

The exhibit is marked, offered, and admitted on proper foundation, but the actual exhibit is not shown to or provided to the jury for their exhibit books. Instead, the relevant portions of recorded recollection are read to the jury, so those portions are merely heard, just like the testimony that they are meant to replace.

7.4 Opposing Party Statements

Documents containing statements by the opposing party (admissions) will be received on a showing of relevance alone. Opposing party statements are relevant statements by the opposing party to the case, made at any time (presumably all the way back to the natural person's coming of rational age or to a fictive person's creation (like the date of incorporation of a company). The statements might have been made twenty years earlier in social conversation, or they may be statements made in interrogatory responses, pleadings, depositions, or opening statement; if they are relevant (and do not violate Rule 403 because of some unfair prejudice, confusion, or other policy-based reason for exclusion), they will be received. Sometimes, statements made in court or in filings by the opposing counsel or party are called "judicial admissions." If your jurisdiction recognizes such a category, statements made in pleadings, interrogatory answers, stipulations, and open court are "judicial admissions" and are entitled to conclusive effect; they may not be contradicted by declarations, documents, or testimony from the party originally making them. Other admissions, sometimes collectively called, "evidentiary admissions," do not normally have such conclusive effect.[1] Party admissions are occasionally, and mistakenly, called "admissions against interest," and statements against interest are also often mistakenly called "admissions." The differences between the two categories of statements, clear from a comparison of Rule 801(d)(2) and 804(b)(3), are important:

---

1. Statements made by designees in FED. R. CIV. P. 30(b)(6) depositions of an organization are said by some courts to have binding effect; other courts treat them as simple party statements; where the questions in such depositions have gone beyond the specifications attached to the notice of deposition, the related answers may not be seen as admissions at all.

- opposing party statements are only made by parties and their representatives or designees, while statements against interest can be made by anyone;

- party statements do not depend upon the unavailability of the party to the lawsuit (obviously), but statements against interest will *only* be received when the declarant is unavailable;

- party statements might even have been to the advantage of the party when the statement was made, but statements against interest must (in most states and the federal system) have been against the penal, pecuniary or property interests of the declarant when made;

- party statements do not require the party making the statement to have a foundation for making the admission. It is enough that the party said it and now needs to explain it.

7.5 Self-Authenticating Evidence

Some items of evidence are self-authenticating and require no testimony to demonstrate that they are what their proponent claims. "Self-authentication" is based on two principles: first, the unlikelihood of forgery and, second, the need to get on with life (and the resolution of this lawsuit). Rule 902 presents the concept of self-authentication, under which some exhibits are considered so likely to be genuine—that is, to be what their proponent says they are—that a rebuttable presumption of authenticity is attached to them. A nonexhaustive list of examples is provided by the rule, and it includes such exhibits as those bearing trade inscriptions (like soft-drink cans and cartons of asbestos insulation), letterhead, newspapers, domestic public documents under seal, and commercial instruments. The unifying principle among these examples is the extremely low likelihood of forgery, coupled with the need to spend trial time on issues more seriously in dispute. Thus, these items will be presumed authentic unless the opponent to the admission comes forward with evidence suggesting the presumption is inappropriate. After a showing of relevance, if the item is received by the court based on the presumption of authenticity, the jury could still conclude that it is not the genuine article. Remember, as mentioned earlier, receipt in evidence requires a finding by the court only that a reasonable jury *could* find that the article is what the proponent says it is; not that it *must* be that item.

7.6 Learned Treatises

Learned treatises will be admitted if the material cited is relevant and the authority is reliable; however, as a substitute for testimony (from the absent author), the treatise portion is treated just like a document containing past recollection recorded. Under Rule 803(18), the foundation of the reliability of the authority can be based on testimony by your expert, the opposing expert, or judicial notice. Your expert can lay that foundation easily enough by direct testimony that the authority is considered reliable. ("Authority" here, as a technical matter, refers to the particular publication being presented, but in practice courts do not always distinguish between the author and the work. As a result, if the author is eminent and well-respected, his works are likely to be considered "authoritative and reliable.") Some works are so widely recognized as authoritative that the court is likely to take judicial notice of that fact.

Examples might be a Rand McNally map of New Jersey highways; or the Oxford English Dictionary; or the Rolling Stone Album Guide. A final way to establish the authoritative nature of a "learned treatise" is through the testimony of the opposing expert.

Like any other question on cross-examination, you should be able to prove the answer before asking this question, but a careful deposition can provide the necessary ammunition. A direct attack at the deposition may not obtain what you need, but questions like, "What books do you recommend to your students who want to do further reading?" or "What sources do you consult when you prepare your lectures or write your articles?" may give you a list of learned treatise candidates. Ask about books written by the expert in the office next door to the opposing expert. Since they drink coffee, play bridge, and have lunch together, it is unlikely that the expert witness will deny that his colleague's book is authoritative. When you find something in the authority that contradicts or favorably explains away the opposing expert's opinion, lay the foundation by reminding the court of your expert's testimony or use the opposing expert's deposition as the foundation; ask the court's permission to read from the article or text, to remind the court of the source of the "reliable authority" foundation; identify the section to be read; and, in compliance with the rule, call it to the witness's attention by reading it aloud. By that reading, the excerpt is included in the record; the paper, book, or tape is not given to the jury because it takes the place of the oral testimony of the expert author.

7.7 Summary Exhibits

Summary exhibits are as admissible as the data that they summarize—and no more. Under Rule 1006, the "voluminous underlying data" should not be offered in evidence; it merely has to be admissible. If the summary exhibit, as part of an expert's testimony, displays inadmissible material that is technically appropriate for an expert to rely on because it is the basis for her day-to-day work, the exhibit should still not be admitted unless such data itself constitutes a business record. Under Rule 403, the exhibit should be excluded because it could create a serious potential for confusing the jurors about the proper consideration and weight to be given the inadmissible material displayed as part of the summary of the material. An exhibit is not admissible merely because it is a summary; the underlying material itself must be admissible, even if it is never offered.

CHAPTER EIGHT

EXHIBITS DIVULGED OR OBTAINED AS PART OF MANDATORY "VOLUNTARY" PRETRIAL DISCLOSURES AND OTHER DISCOVERY

8.1 Problems with Voluntary Disclosure

Documents to be disclosed pursuant to Federal Rule of Civil Procedure 26(a) are supposed to be those that "relate to the issues" in the case. This rule was intended to eliminate discovery problems, but it really has not operated that way. First of all, it leaves to the judgment of the disclosing attorney the decision as to what "relates" to what. Second, the adverse parties are likely to disagree on what the issues are and what documents should have been disclosed, thereby introducing another source of pretrial motions practice. As a result, the initial disclosures by the attorneys are likely to be incomplete and give rise to time-consuming challenges, or, more likely, to discovery as broad in total as that which occurred before the disclosure procedure was adopted.

8.2   Exhibit Requests

Properly drafted exhibit requests can obtain useful opposing party statements. The act of returning an exhibit in response to a document request, or an interrogatory, or as part of an initial voluntary disclosure, itself constitutes a statement regarding portions of the foundation for the exhibit. For example, if a document request calls for the production of "all documents that show profits earned between May 2005 and May 2006," then the return of twelve documents in response constitutes a party statement of two facts: that the twelve documents are relevant to profits in that period, and that the opposing party has no access to (or "custody or control" of) any other documents that are relevant to profits during that time. Therefore, in discovery, do not ask only for "documents sufficient to show," because you do not obtain the benefit of this second party statement; ask for "all documents that relate." Parties will often provide documents in response to an inter-rogatory, as they are allowed to do by the rules. That response then constitutes a statement that those documents answer the interrogatory, i.e., that they are relevant to the subject. By provid-ing exhibits in an initial voluntary disclosure, the opposing party is, at the least, stating that those documents are relevant to the issues; technically, the party is conceding that the produced docu-ments are all the documents that the party has that are relevant to the issues, but you will likely find it difficult to persuade a court to apply the language of the voluntary disclosure rule quite so strictly (albeit logically).

CHAPTER NINE

THE MECHANICS OF PRETRIAL LISTINGS AND PRETRIAL RULINGS ON EXHIBITS

9.1 Before the Final Pretrial Conference

Typical pretrial standing orders or local rules require exhibits to be identified, exchanged, and offered before the final pretrial conference. Most judges do not want to take trial time to hear arguments about foundation for exhibits; therefore they require exchange and objection to occur prior to trial and will not hear objections later that could have been made pretrial. However, objections based on relevance and the various policies embodied in Rule 403—such as cumulativeness, confusion, unfair prejudice, and waste of time—will often be deferred until trial, because the judge needs the advantage of context to make a proper ruling. Nevertheless, the objections should be stated pretrial so they are not waived.

9.2 Pretrial Objections

Objections to exhibits that are made and over-ruled at pretrial should normally be renewed at trial, at least in the form of a proffer made on the record, out of the hearing of the jury. The court may state in pretrial on the record or in a written order that it will not allow exhibit offers to be renewed at trial if the objection was sustained during pretrial; the court may also state that it will not allow overruled objections to be restated during trial when the exhibit is introduced. If there is no such preclusive ruling, the objecting attorney should renew the objection when the exhibit is offered at trial. The objection might be stated when the jury is out, during a bench conference, or in a morning or evening housekeeping session, but it should be in the presence of the reporter so that it is on the record. It is true that some judges get testy about attorneys restating offers or objections that the judge thought were completely and properly overruled at pretrial; if the judge seems perturbed, explain that you are concerned about having an adequate record and do not intend to re-argue the ruling—you just want to make certain that it is clearly contained in the record and not waived.

9.3   Motions in Limine

Motions in limine are used to get advance rulings of admissibility as well as advance rulings of inadmissibility. It is perhaps a common misunderstanding, based on a mistranslation of the phrase "in limine" as meaning "to limit," when it actually means, "at the threshold" of the courtroom or chambers. If you anticipate a challenge to an exhibit, and it is sufficiently important to the flow of your case that you do not want to wait until trial to find out whether it is going to be admitted, ask for an in limine ruling. Of course, if the court has scheduled an "exhibit day" during the pretrial sessions, you can obtain your ruling at that time. However, there are judges who prefer to postpone routine exhibit rulings until they come up at trial. When you are in front of one of these judges, it is appropriate to request in limine rulings on important exhibits.[1]

9.4 Exhibit Book

From the activities and your handling of matters during pretrial, the court will form an early impression about your evidentiary competence and organization; therefore, use an "exhibit book" or "trial notebook" during pretrial and trial arguments on exhibits. For the exhibit day, if you are dealing with 200 to 300 exhibits, put your copies in one or two notebooks, in numerical order. If your opponent has conceded the admissibility of the exhibit, indicate that at the top in some bright color. For those exhibits for which admissibility has not been conceded, write "OPRAH" vertically

---

1. Incidentally, off the topic of exhibits, under *Daubert*, when it is difficult to forecast in advance whether a particular judge will find a foundation to be adequate for an expert's testimony, a request for an in limine ruling of admissibility may be essential, and that request should include the expert's exhibits as well. The presentation supporting that request for a ruling may include live testimony, under the procedures of FED. R. EVID. 104(c).

at the top of the first page of each exhibit.[2] Then consider how you would respond to any objection on any of those elements of foundation and make a note opposite the element.

9.5 Keeping Track of Your Objections to Opponents Exhibits

Use the same OPRAH notation to keep track of your objections to your opponent's exhibits, right at the top or in the margin of your copy of the exhibit. In your notations across from the OPRAH element, refer to the federal or state rule of evidence that supports your objection or your response to your opponent's objection. If you have the rule numbers right at your fingertips, the judge will come to trust you and rely on your evidentiary arguments.

9.6 Bench Brief

Present a "bench brief" to the court if an evidentiary argument on an exhibit is sufficiently important. A bench brief is a three- or

---

2. *See* section 1.1 for a description of the OPRAH elements.

four-paragraph, one- or two-page statement of the admissibility issue, the two leading cases in your jurisdiction on a particular point, and one paragraph of your application of that law to the issue. It must be this short because it is intended to guide and persuade the court during the next recess. When the judge is about to rule, and you fear that the ruling will be adverse to your position, offer her your bench brief, asking if she would consider it at the next break before ruling. Give a copy to opposing counsel, of course. On some points that come up frequently, like the adequacy of a foundation for expert testimony, you might have previously prepared bench briefs that you update regularly and then use from trial to trial.

9.7 Trial Notebook

At trial, arrange your trial notebook so that your notes on foundation and OPRAH are visible, perhaps on the left-hand side, when you turn to the next document to be considered.

CHAPTER TEN

THE NEXT LEVEL OF PERSUASION WITH EXHIBITS

10.1 Persuasive Foundation

Every exhibit has both a legal and a persuasive foundation. Remember to emphasize the persuasive foundation for your exhibits. The persuasive foundation consists of a set of questions for the witness that will allow her to explain to the jury how the exhibit relates to key issues.

Too often the lawyers get to the exhibit too early, suggesting that the exhibit is the important portion of the story, and they miss the greater importance of activities of which the exhibit is only a part. For example, an exhibit may merely corroborate an important event, like the fact that a telephone call was made in which goods were ordered. The exhibit must not overshadow the importance and relatively greater drama of the witness's memory of actually making the telephone call and placing the order.

Sometimes the context is independently persuasive. For example, you should not interrupt a police officer who is telling what he saw when he arrived at the scene of an accident, just when he is about to tell about the condition of your client's injuries. Your question like, "Officer, did you prepare a diagram which shows the scene as you found it?" could wait until the officer had described how your client looked—bloodied and unconscious. Or a lawyer may miss the opportunity to give additional emphasis to a point by having it told twice. If the witness can describe an event orally, with drama, then the lawyer can go back over it with a document, providing more detail the second time.

Finally, even the technical foundation should not be rushed. If a document is a business record, use the Federal Rules of Evidence to let the jurors in on the persuasive nature of the foundation. By asking about the importance of records to a particular business, by asking the witness to tell the jurors about who uses the records and why the business needs the records and the care with which the records were kept, the persuasive foundation will be laid simultaneously with the technical foundation.

10.2 No Walking and Talking

Do not "walk and talk" during important testimony on exhibits. In the theatre, when one character is delivering an important line or speech, the other actors are supposed to refrain from any activity that would distract the audience's attention; otherwise, they are guilty of "upstaging" the actor during the scene, or "walking on his lines." In court, when you are handling your own exhibits, remember this same rule. It is okay to walk and talk when you are not saying anything important; for example, when you are delivering copies of the exhibit to the opponent, the court, and the witness. When you are asking substantive questions about an exhibit, however, you should stand still; when your witness is speaking about an exhibit, stand still; when you have just handed an important exhibit to the jury, and you want them to see the clarity with which it makes your point, stand still. Otherwise, your movement around the courtroom will make your audience think that they need to watch you, that you might be doing something more interesting than the exhibit.

10.3 Value Your Exhibits

Your exhibits are gold, and your opponents are dross. Many attorneys carry all documents around the courtroom as though they were as valuable as a brown lunch bag—papers bunched in their fists, arms dangling casually at their sides, eyes on the witness or court. That may be a fine way to carry an opponent's exhibit; the implicit message is that the exhibit is not worth any more attention or care than that; those exhibits are the dross, the metallic impurities that are discarded during the smelting of gold. But with your own exhibits, treat each sheet as though it was engraved on gold foil, as though it had substantial weight, as though each time you looked at it you were once again impressed with its significance. Hold your exhibit in two hands as you carry it across the courtroom and return it to your table or folder as though you cared about keeping it organized and undamaged. With your most important exhibits (just a few), keep your copies in envelopes, and put them back into those envelopes after you ask your questions. Then, during closing argument, you can take them out of the envelopes again, and the jury will remember that these are the important exhibits.

10.4   Get and Deal with the Bad

Observe the "get the bad news at the deposition" rule. Some attorneys find what they think is good information in documents during pretrial and then shy away from asking about that information during deposition because they do not want to give the witness a chance to explain it away. But if the witness is going to try to explain the document away, you had better hear that explanation at the deposition so you plan for dealing with that explanation at trial. If you do not hear the explanation until trial, it will likely be too late to do anything about it.

10.5   Tell a Story

Tell a story with the exhibits. Especially during opening and closing speeches, you must use the exhibits to tell the story, to support the theme you have chosen for the case. If the documents do not directly support the theme, then they necessarily detract from it. Often, there are too many documents (see the next rule) or they are not well-organized (not chronological or not sufficiently related to the point being made). As a test of the effectiveness of the organization and choice of documents, arrange them on a storyboard of their own and ask a focus group or a group of non-attorneys in the office to review them for fifteen minutes and report to you on the meaning that they have gained from the collection. If it is not substantially in line with your theme and theory, rethink your selection and organization.

10.6 The Fourteen-Document Rule

Use the "fourteen-document" rule. In every trial, no matter the subject matter, there are no more than fourteen documents that will determine the jury's or judge's decision. You may need to massage ten or a hundred times that many documents to obtain the information you will present; but the jury and judge cannot make intelligent use of hundreds of documents in coming to a decision. Instead, they will make their own selection of what they think are the most important documents, or the most reliable documents, or the documents that best stand for a larger mass of evidence. If you emphasize the fourteen documents that tell your story, illustrate your points, or sum up your theme and theory, the jury and judge may accept your selection. Of course, the fourteen may actually be seven, or twenty-four, but it will not be fifty, and it will certainly not be fourteen hundred or fourteen thousand. Get your experts to select and identify representative documents; ask them to create summary exhibits; look for simplified proxies for complicated bundles. If you present the evidence in a way that the jurors and judge find easier to handle and understand, they will follow and accept your proof.

INDEX